T0072803

THE HIDDEN WORDS
OF BAHÁ'U'LLÁH

Bahá'u'lláh (1817–92) was born in Tehran, Iran, the son of a wealthy nobleman and landowner. An early follower of the Bab (1819–50), he suffered religious persecution, torture and imprisonment before being exiled with his family to Baghdad, Iraq, in 1853. In 1863 he announced that he was the Promised One anticipated by the Bab, thus marking the birth of the Bahá'í Faith, now – almost one and a half centuries later – the second most widespread of the world religions. The same year he was transferred by the Ottoman authorities first to Edirne, in Turkey, and in 1868 to the prison-city of Acre, Palestine, where he spent the remaining twenty-four years of his life. He died in 1892 at the age of seventy-four.

The writings of Bahá'u'lláh amount to more than one hundred volumes of commentaries, letters, prayers and teachings, in both Persian and Arabic, on a broad range of theological, philosophical, ethical and social issues. Only a proportion of his works have so far been translated into English. Of these, his major writings include *The Hidden Words* (1857–8), *The Book of Certitude* (1862), *The Seven Valleys* (1863), a series of proclamations to the kings, queens and rulers of the day in which he called upon them to reconcile their differences and establish peace and justice in the world (c. 1867–9), and *The Most Holy Book* (1873).

THE HIDDEN WORDS OF BAHÁ'U'LLÁH

Translated by Shoghi Effendi

ONEWORLD

THE HIDDEN WORDS OF BAHÁ'U'LLÁH

Translated by Shoghi Effendi
First Oneworld edition © Oneworld Publications 1986
Reissued 2004, reprinted 2007 and 2012

All rights reserved
Copyright under Berne Convention
A CIP record for this title is available
from the British Library

ISBN 978-1-85168-349-9 (pb)
978-1-85168-352-9 (hb)
Cover illustration by Bob Haberfield
Printed and bound in by Nørhaven, Denmark

Oneworld Publications
185 Banbury Road
Oxford OX2 7AR, England
www.oneworld-publications.com

1858, Iraq. Walking along the banks of the River Tigris, wrapt in meditation, Bahá'u'lláh – prophet-founder of the Bahá'í Faith – reflected on the eternal relationship between God and man, on the purpose of life, and on the obstacles that lie before man in the path of spiritual perfection. Out of such profound contemplation poured forth the inspiration for this absorbing collection of short meditational verses, in whose brief lines may be found a distillation of those spiritual truths that have been the central inspirational force behind all the religious traditions of the past. George Townshend, sometime Canon of St Patrick's Cathedral, Dublin and Archdeacon of Clonfert, an eminent scholar, described *The Hidden Words* thus:

> It has the sweep, the force, the freshness of an original work. It is rich with imagery, laden with thought, throbbing with emotion. Even at the remove of a translation one feels the strength and majesty of the style and marvels at the character of a writing which combines so warm and tender a loving kindness with such dignity and elevation.

Revolving around man's constant struggle to acquire spiritual vision and divine perfections, the verses are interwoven throughout with loving counsels, gentle remonstrations and words of wisdom, the whole borne up as if on wings by the most intense and steadfast spirituality. From the opening lines the reader is captivated by the vision and drawn unprotesting from this earthly world to the mystic realms above where he may find at last an expression of the deepest impulses of his heart and mind. Over one hundred and fifty verses, its exquisite beauty, majestic prose and breadth of vision lend this small volume a timeless and universal quality – an outstanding contribution to the world's religious literature.

Bahá'u'lláh, the author of *The Hidden Words*, was born in 1817 of an ancient and noble Persian family. Like the founders of other religions before him, he suffered relentless persecution at the hands of both the clergy and the state in the land of his birth, and his cause was rejected by his own countrymen. Stripped of all his possessions, he was imprisoned, tortured and, in 1853, exiled from his native land, to Baghdad, Iraq. The following year, he began a two-year sojourn in the mountains of Kurdistan, withdrawing from the world to live the simple life of solitary contemplation in a cave, where his fame as a mystic and spiritual teacher soon spread throughout the area. After his return to Baghdad, Bahá'u'lláh wrote *The Hidden Words* (1857–8), his greatest ethical work. In 1868 the Persian authorities delivered him into the hands of the Ottomans, who consigned him to life-imprisonment in the penal colony of Acre, Palestine, a gaol reserved for the Empire's lowest criminals. After almost forty years of unimaginable hardship in exile and confinement, it was here that he died at the age of seventy-four, still a prisoner.

Bahá'u'lláh wrote extensively in Persian and Arabic on a broad range of subjects, addressing not only those timeless theological and philosophical themes that have plagued humanity since antiquity – such as God, soul and the purpose of life – but also the issues that have preoccupied present-day thinkers such as equality of the sexes, harmony of science and religion and the need for unity and a global order. In addition to writing on theological issues, social and moral teachings, and mysticism, he penned many prayers and meditations for devotional use, of which *The Hidden Words* is perhaps the best known. Described as a guidebook to the spiritual life, it provides inspiring counsels for a daily spiritual practice to bring the soul closer to God. For many years only a few treasured manuscripts of this book existed, passed from hand to hand and carefully concealed from those who opposed the infant religion. Now, however, this profoundly edifying little volume has been translated from its original Persian and Arabic into sixty-nine languages, and is loved and learned by heart throughout the world.

From the Arabic

HE IS THE GLORY OF GLORIES

This is that which hath descended from the realm of glory, uttered by the tongue of power and might, and revealed unto the Prophets of old. We have taken the inner essence thereof and clothed it in the garment of brevity, as a token of grace unto the righteous, that they may stand faithful unto the Covenant of God, may fulfil in their lives His trust, and in the realm of spirit obtain the gem of Divine virtue.

1

O SON OF SPIRIT!

My first counsel is this: Possess a pure, kindly and radiant heart, that thine may be a sovereignty ancient, imperishable and everlasting.

2

O SON OF SPIRIT!

The best beloved of all things in My sight is Justice; turn not away therefrom if thou desirest Me, and neglect it not that I may confide in thee. By its aid thou shalt see with thine own eyes and not through the eyes of others, and shalt know of thine own knowledge and not through the knowledge of thy neighbour. Ponder this in thy heart, how it behoveth thee to be. Verily justice is My gift to thee and the sign of My loving-kindness. Set it then before thine eyes.

3

O SON OF MAN!

Veiled in My immemorial being and in the ancient eternity of My essence, I knew My love for thee; therefore I created thee, have engraved on thee Mine image and revealed to thee My beauty.

4

O SON OF MAN!

I loved thy creation, hence I created thee. Wherefore, do thou love Me, that I may name thy name and fill thy soul with the spirit of life.

5

O SON OF BEING!

Love Me, that I may love thee. If thou lovest Me not, My love can in no wise reach thee. Know this, O servant.

6

O SON OF BEING!

Thy Paradise is My love; thy heavenly home, reunion with Me. Enter therein and tarry not. This is that which hath been destined for thee in Our kingdom above and Our exalted Dominion.

7

O SON OF MAN!

If thou lovest Me, turn away from thyself; and if thou seekest My pleasure, regard not thine own; that thou mayest die in Me and I may eternally live in thee.

8

O SON OF SPIRIT!

There is no peace for thee save by renouncing thyself and turning unto Me; for it behoveth thee to glory in My name, not in thine own; to put thy trust in Me and not in thyself, since I desire to be loved alone and above all that is.

9

O SON OF BEING!

My love is My stronghold; he that entereth therein is safe and secure, and he that turneth away shall surely stray and perish.

10

O SON OF UTTERANCE!

Thou art My stronghold; enter therein that thou mayest abide in safety. My love is in thee, know it, that thou mayest find Me near unto thee.

11

O SON OF BEING!

Thou art My lamp and My light is in thee. Get thou from it thy radiance and seek none other than Me. For I have created thee rich and have bountifully shed My favour upon thee.

12

O SON OF BEING!

With the hands of power I made thee and with the fingers of strength I created thee; and within thee have I placed the essence of My light. Be thou content with it and seek naught else, for My work is perfect and My command is binding. Question it not, nor have a doubt thereof.

13

O SON OF SPIRIT!

I created thee rich, why dost thou bring thyself down to poverty? Noble I made thee, wherewith dost thou abase thyself? Out of the essence of knowledge I gave thee being, why seekest thou enlightenment from anyone beside Me? Out of the clay of love I moulded thee, how dost thou busy thyself with another? Turn thy sight unto thyself, that thou mayest find Me standing within thee, mighty, powerful and self-subsisting.

14

O SON OF MAN!

Thou art My dominion and My dominion perisheth not, wherefore fearest thou thy perishing? Thou art My light and My light shall never be extinguished, why dost thou dread extinction? Thou art My glory and My glory fadeth not; thou art My robe and My robe shall never be outworn. Abide then in thy love for Me, that thou mayest find Me in the realm of glory.

15

O SON OF UTTERANCE!

Turn thy face unto Mine and renounce all save Me; for My sovereignty endureth and My dominion perisheth not. If thou seekest another than Me, yea, if thou searchest the universe for evermore, thy quest will be in vain.

16

O SON OF LIGHT!

Forget all save Me and commune with My spirit. This is of the essence of My command, therefore turn unto it.

17

O SON OF MAN!

Be thou content with Me and seek no other helper.

For none but Me can ever suffice thee.

18

O SON OF SPIRIT!

Ask not of Me that which We desire not for thee,

then be content with what We have ordained for thy sake, for this is that

which profiteth thee, if therewith thou dost content thyself.

19

O SON OF THE WONDROUS VISION!

I have breathed within thee a breath of My own Spirit, that thou mayest be My lover. Why hast thou forsaken Me and sought a beloved other than Me?

20

O SON OF SPIRIT!

My claim on thee is great, it cannot be forgotten. My grace to thee is plenteous, it cannot be veiled. My love has made in thee its home, it cannot be concealed. My light is manifest to thee, it cannot be obscured.

21

O SON OF MAN!

Upon the tree of effulgent glory I have hung for thee the choicest fruits, wherefore hast thou turned away and contented thyself with that which is less good? Return then unto that which is better for thee in the realm on high.

22

O SON OF SPIRIT!

Noble have I created thee, yet thou hast abased thyself. Rise then unto that for which thou wast created.

23

O SON OF THE SUPREME!

To the eternal I call thee, yet thou dost seek that which perisheth. What hath made thee turn away from Our desire and seek thine own?

24

O SON OF MAN!

Transgress not thy limits, nor claim that which beseemeth thee not. Prostrate thyself before the countenance of thy God, the Lord of might and power.

25

O SON OF SPIRIT!

Vaunt not thyself over the poor, for I lead him on his way and behold thee in thy evil plight and confound thee for evermore.

26

O SON OF BEING!

How couldst thou forget thine own faults and busy thyself with the faults of others? Whoso doeth this is accursed of Me.

27

O SON OF MAN!

Breathe not the sins of others so long as thou art thyself a sinner. Shouldst thou transgress this command, accursed wouldst thou be, and to this I bear witness.

28

O SON OF SPIRIT!

Know thou of a truth: He that biddeth men be just and himself committeth iniquity is not of Me, even though he bear My name.

29

O SON OF BEING!

Ascribe not to any soul that which thou wouldst not have ascribed to thee, and say not that which thou doest not. This is My command unto thee, do thou observe it.

30

O SON OF MAN!

Deny not My servant should he ask anything from thee, for his face is My face; be then abashed before Me.

31

O SON OF BEING!

Bring thyself to account each day ere thou art
summoned to a reckoning; for death, unheralded, shall come upon thee
and thou shalt be called to give account for thy deeds.

32

O SON OF THE SUPREME!

I have made death a messenger of joy to thee.
Wherefore dost thou grieve? I made the light to shed on thee its splendour.
Why dost thou veil thyself therefrom?

33

O SON OF SPIRIT!

With the joyful tidings of light I hail thee: rejoice! To the court of holiness I summon thee; abide therein that thou mayest live in peace for evermore.

34

O SON OF SPIRIT!

The spirit of holiness beareth unto thee the joyful tidings of reunion; wherefore dost thou grieve? The spirit of power confirmeth thee in His cause; why dost thou veil thyself? The light of His countenance doth lead thee; how canst thou go astray?

35

O SON OF MAN!

Sorrow not save that thou art far from Us.

Rejoice not save that thou art drawing near and returning unto Us.

36

O SON OF MAN!

Rejoice in the gladness of thine heart, that thou

mayest be worthy to meet Me and to mirror forth My beauty.

37

O SON OF MAN!

Divest not thyself of My beauteous robe, and forfeit not thy portion from My wondrous fountain, lest thou shouldst thirst for evermore.

38

O SON OF BEING!

Walk in My statutes for love of Me and deny thyself that which thou desirest if thou seekest My pleasure.

39

O SON OF MAN!

Neglect not My commandments if thou lovest My beauty, and forget not My counsels if thou wouldst attain My good pleasure.

40

O SON OF MAN!

Wert thou to speed through the immensity of space and traverse the expanse of heaven, yet thou wouldst find no rest save in submission to Our command and humbleness before Our Face.

41

O SON OF MAN!

Magnify My cause that I may reveal unto thee the mysteries of My greatness and shine upon thee with the light of eternity.

42

O SON OF MAN!

Humble thyself before Me, that I may graciously visit thee. Arise for the triumph of My cause, that while yet on earth thou mayest obtain the victory.

43

O SON OF BEING!

Make mention of Me on My earth, that in My heaven I may remember thee, thus shall Mine eyes and thine be solaced.

44

O SON OF THE THRONE!

Thy hearing is My hearing, hear thou therewith. Thy sight is My sight, do thou see therewith, that in thine inmost soul thou mayest testify unto My exalted sanctity, and I within Myself may bear witness unto an exalted station for thee.

45

O SON OF BEING!

Seek a martyr's death in My path, content with My pleasure and thankful for that which I ordain, that thou mayest repose with Me beneath the canopy of majesty behind the tabernacle of glory.

46

O SON OF MAN!

Ponder and reflect. Is it thy wish to die upon thy bed, or to shed thy life-blood on the dust, a martyr in My path, and so become the manifestation of My command and the revealer of My light in the highest paradise? Judge thou aright, O servant!

47

O SON OF MAN!

By My beauty! To tinge thy hair with thy blood is greater in My sight than the creation of the universe and the light of both worlds. Strive then to attain this, O servant!

48

O SON OF MAN!

For everything there is a sign. The sign of love is fortitude under My decree and patience under My trials.

49

O SON OF MAN!

The true lover yearneth for tribulation even as doth the rebel for forgiveness and the sinful for mercy.

50

O SON OF MAN!

If adversity befall thee not in My path, how canst thou walk in the ways of them that are content with My pleasure? If trials afflict thee not in thy longing to meet Me, how wilt thou attain the light in thy love for My beauty?

51

O SON OF MAN!

My calamity is My providence, outwardly it is fire and vengeance, but inwardly it is light and mercy. Hasten thereunto that thou mayest become an eternal light and an immortal spirit. This is My command unto thee, do thou observe it.

52

O SON OF MAN!

Should prosperity befall thee, rejoice not, and should abasement come upon thee, grieve not, for both shall pass away and be no more.

53

O SON OF BEING!

If poverty overtake thee, be not sad; for in time the Lord of wealth shall visit thee. Fear not abasement, for glory shall one day rest on thee.

54

O SON OF BEING!

If thine heart be set upon this eternal, imperishable dominion, and this ancient, everlasting life, forsake this mortal and fleeting sovereignty.

55

O SON OF BEING!

Busy not thyself with this world, for with fire We test the gold, and with gold We test Our servants.

56

O SON OF MAN!

Thou dost wish for gold and I desire thy freedom from it. Thou thinkest thyself rich in its possession, and I recognize thy wealth in thy sanctity therefrom. By My life! This is My knowledge, and that is thy fancy; how can My way accord with thine?

57

O SON OF MAN!

Bestow My wealth upon My poor, that in heaven thou mayest draw from stores of unfading splendour and treasures of imperishable glory. But by My life! To offer up thy soul is a more glorious thing couldst thou but see with Mine eye.

58

O SON OF MAN!

The temple of being is My throne; cleanse it of all things, that there I may be established and there I may abide.

59

O SON OF BEING!

Thy heart is My home; sanctify it for My descent.

Thy spirit is My place of revelation; cleanse it for My manifestation.

60

O SON OF MAN!

Put thy hand into My bosom, that I may rise

above thee, radiant and resplendent.

61

O SON OF MAN!

Ascend unto My heaven, that thou mayest obtain the joy of reunion, and from the chalice of imperishable glory quaff the peerless wine.

62

O SON OF MAN!

Many a day hath passed over thee whilst thou hast busied thyself with thy fancies and idle imaginings. How long art thou to slumber on thy bed? Lift up thy head from slumber, for the Sun hath risen to the zenith, haply it may shine upon thee with the light of beauty.

63

O SON OF MAN!

The light hath shone on thee from the horizon of the sacred Mount and the spirit of enlightenment hath breathed in the Sinai of thy heart. Wherefore, free thyself from the veils of idle fancies and enter into My court, that thou mayest be fit for everlasting life and worthy to meet Me. Thus may death not come upon thee, neither weariness nor trouble.

64

O SON OF MAN!

My eternity is My creation, I have created it for thee. Make it the garment of thy temple. My unity is My handiwork, I have wrought it for thee; clothe thyself therewith, that thou mayest be to all eternity the revelation of My everlasting being.

65

O SON OF MAN!

My majesty is My gift to thee, and My grandeur the token of My mercy unto thee. That which beseemeth Me none shall understand, nor can anyone recount. Verily, I have preserved it in My hidden storehouses and in the treasuries of My command, as a sign of My loving-kindness unto My servants and My mercy unto My people.

66

O CHILDREN OF THE DIVINE AND INVISIBLE ESSENCE!

Ye shall be hindered from loving Me and souls shall be perturbed as they make mention of Me. For minds cannot grasp Me nor hearts contain Me.

67

O SON OF BEAUTY!

By My spirit and by My favour! By My mercy and by My beauty! All that I have revealed unto thee with the tongue of power, and have written for thee with the pen of might, hath been in accordance with thy capacity and understanding, not with My state and the melody of My voice.

68

O CHILDREN OF MEN!

Know ye not why We created you all from the same dust? That no one should exalt himself over the other. Ponder at all times in your hearts how ye were created. Since We have created you all from one same substance it is incumbent on you to be even as one soul, to walk with the same feet, eat with the same mouth and dwell in the same land, that from your inmost being, by your deeds and actions, the signs of oneness and the essence of detachment may be made manifest. Such is My counsel to you, O concourse of light! Heed ye this counsel that ye may obtain the fruit of holiness from the tree of wondrous glory.

69

O YE SONS OF SPIRIT!

Ye are My treasury, for in you I have treasured the pearls of My mysteries and the gems of My knowledge. Guard them from the strangers amidst My servants and from the ungodly amongst My people.

70

O SON OF HIM THAT STOOD BY HIS OWN ENTITY IN THE KINGDOM OF HIS SELF!

Know thou, that I have wafted unto thee all the fragrances of holiness, have fully revealed to thee My word, have perfected through thee My bounty and have desired for thee that which I have desired for My Self. Be then content with My pleasure and thankful unto me.

71

O SON OF MAN!

Write all that We have revealed unto thee with the ink of light upon the tablet of thy spirit. Should this not be in thy power, then make thine ink of the essence of thy heart. If this thou canst not do, then write with that crimson ink that hath been shed in My path. Sweeter indeed is this to Me than all else, that its light may endure for ever.

From the Persian

In the Name of the Lord of Utterance, the Mighty.

I

O YE PEOPLE THAT HAVE MINDS TO KNOW AND EARS TO HEAR!

The first call of the Beloved is this: O mystic nightingale! Abide not but in the rose-garden of the spirit. O messenger of the Solomon of love! Seek thou no shelter except in the Sheba of the well-beloved, and O immortal phoenix! dwell not save on the mount of faithfulness. Therein is thy habitation, if on the wings of thy soul thou soarest to the realm of the infinite and seekest to attain thy goal.

2

O SON OF SPIRIT!

The bird seeketh its nest; the nightingale the charm of the rose; whilst those birds, the hearts of men, content with transient dust, have strayed far from their eternal nest, and with eyes turned towards the slough of heedlessness are bereft of the glory of the divine presence. Alas! How strange and pitiful; for a mere cupful, they have turned away from the billowing seas of the Most High, and remained far from the most effulgent horizon.

3

O FRIEND!

In the garden of thy heart plant naught but the rose of love, and from the nightingale of affection and desire loosen not thy hold. Treasure the companionship of the righteous and eschew all fellowship with the ungodly.

4

O SON OF JUSTICE!

Whither can a lover go but to the land of his beloved? and what seeker findeth rest away from his heart's desire? To the true lover reunion is life, and separation is death. His breast is void of patience and his heart hath no peace. A myriad lives he would forsake to hasten to the abode of his beloved.

5

O SON OF DUST!

Verily I say unto thee: Of all men the most negligent is he that disputeth idly and seeketh to advance himself over his brother. Say, O brethren! Let deeds, not words, be your adorning.

6

O SON OF EARTH!

Know, verily, the heart wherein the least remnant of envy yet lingers, shall never attain My everlasting dominion, nor inhale the sweet savours of holiness breathing from My kingdom of sanctity.

7

O SON OF LOVE!

Thou art but one step away from the glorious heights above and from the celestial tree of love. Take thou one pace and with the next advance into the immortal realm and enter the pavilion of eternity. Give ear then to that which hath been revealed by the pen of glory.

8

O SON OF GLORY!

Be swift in the path of holiness, and enter the heaven of communion with Me. Cleanse thy heart with the burnish of the spirit, and hasten to the court of the Most High.

9

O FLEETING SHADOW!

Pass beyond the baser stages of doubt and rise to the exalted heights of certainty. Open the eye of truth, that thou mayest behold the veilless Beauty and exclaim: Hallowed be the Lord, the most excellent of all creators!

10

O SON OF DESIRE!

Give ear unto this: Never shall mortal eye recognize the everlasting beauty, nor the lifeless heart delight in aught but in the withered bloom. For like seeketh like, and taketh pleasure in the company of its kind.

II

O SON OF DUST!

Blind thine eyes, that thou mayest behold My beauty; stop thine ears, that thou mayest hearken unto the sweet melody of My voice; empty thyself of all learning, that thou mayest partake of My knowledge; and sanctify thyself from riches, that thou mayest obtain a lasting share from the ocean of My eternal wealth. Blind thine eyes, that is, to all save My beauty; stop thine ears to all save My word; empty thyself of all learning save the knowledge of Me; that with a clear vision, a pure heart and an attentive ear thou mayest enter the court of My holiness.

12

O MAN OF TWO VISIONS!

Close one eye and open the other. Close one to the world and all that is therein, and open the other to the hallowed beauty of the Beloved.

13

O MY CHILDREN!

I fear lest, bereft of the melody of the dove of heaven, ye will sink back to the shades of utter loss, and, never having gazed upon the beauty of the rose, return to water and clay.

14

O FRIENDS!

Abandon not the everlasting beauty for a beauty that must die, and set not your affections on this mortal world of dust.

15

O SON OF SPIRIT!

The time cometh when the nightingale of holiness will no longer unfold the inner mysteries and ye will all be bereft of the celestial melody and of the voice from on high.

16

O ESSENCE OF NEGLIGENCE!

Myriads of mystic tongues find utterance in one speech, and myriads of hidden mysteries are revealed in a single melody; yet, alas, there is no ear to hear, nor heart to understand.

17

O COMRADES!

The gates that open on the Placeless stand wide and the habitation of the loved one is adorned with the lovers' blood, yet all but a few remain bereft of this celestial city, and even of these few, none but the smallest handful hath been found with a pure heart and sanctified spirit.

18

O YE DWELLERS IN THE HIGHEST PARADISE!

Proclaim unto the children of assurance that within the realms of holiness, nigh unto the celestial paradise, a new garden hath appeared, round which circle the denizens of the realm on high and the immortal dwellers of the exalted paradise. Strive, then, that ye may attain that station, that ye may unravel the mysteries of love from its wind-flowers and learn the secret of divine and consummate wisdom from its eternal fruits. Solaced are the eyes of them that enter and abide therein!

19

O MY FRIENDS!

Have ye forgotten that true and radiant morn, when in those hallowed and blessed surroundings ye were all gathered in My presence beneath the shade of the tree of life, which is planted in the all-glorious paradise? Awe-struck ye listened as I gave utterance to these three most holy words: O friends! Prefer not your will to Mine, never desire that which I have not desired for you, and approach Me not with lifeless hearts, defiled with worldly desires and cravings. Would ye but sanctify your souls, ye would at this present hour recall that place and those surroundings, and the truth of My utterance should be made evident unto all of you.

In the eighth of the most holy lines, in the fifth Tablet of Paradise, He saith:

20

O YE THAT ARE LYING AS DEAD ON THE COUCH OF HEEDLESSNESS!

Ages have passed and your precious lives are well-nigh ended, yet not a single breath of purity hath reached Our court of holiness from you. Though immersed in the ocean of misbelief, yet with your lips ye profess the one true faith of God. Him whom I abhor ye have loved, and of My foe ye have made a friend. Notwithstanding, ye walk on My earth complacent and self-satisfied, heedless that My earth is weary of you and everything within it shunneth you. Were ye but to open your eyes, ye would, in truth, prefer a myriad griefs unto this joy, and would count death itself better than this life.

21

O MOVING FORM OF DUST!

I desire communion with thee, but thou wouldst put
no trust in Me. The sword of thy rebellion hath felled the tree of
thy hope. At all times I am near unto thee, but thou art ever far from Me.
Imperishable glory I have chosen for thee, yet boundless shame
thou hast chosen for thyself. While there is yet time,
return, and lose not thy chance.

22

O SON OF DESIRE!

The learned and the wise have for long years striven and failed to attain the presence of the All-Glorious; they have spent their lives in search of Him, yet did not behold the beauty of His countenance. Thou without the least effort didst attain thy goal, and without search hast obtained the object of thy quest. Yet, notwithstanding, thou didst remain so wrapt in the veil of self, that thine eyes beheld not the beauty of the Beloved, nor did thy hand touch the hem of His robe. Ye that have eyes, behold and wonder.

23

O DWELLERS IN THE CITY OF LOVE!

Mortal blasts have beset the everlasting candle, and the beauty of the celestial Youth is veiled in the darkness of dust. The chief of the monarchs of love is wronged by the people of tyranny and the dove of holiness lies prisoned in the talons of owls. The dwellers in the pavilion of glory and the celestial concourse bewail and lament, while ye repose in the realm of negligence, and esteem yourselves as of the true friends. How vain are your imaginings!

24

O YE THAT ARE FOOLISH, YET HAVE A NAME TO BE WISE!

Wherefore do ye wear the guise of shepherds, when inwardly ye have become wolves, intent upon My flock? Ye are even as the star, which riseth ere the dawn, and which, though it seem radiant and luminous, leadeth the wayfarers of My city astray into the paths of perdition.

25

O YE SEEMING FAIR YET INWARDLY FOUL!

Ye are like clear but bitter water, which to outward seeming is crystal pure but of which, when tested by the divine Assayer, not a drop is accepted. Yea, the sunbeam falls alike upon the dust and the mirror, yet differ they in reflection even as doth the star from the earth: nay, immeasurable is the difference!

26

O MY FRIEND IN WORD!

Ponder awhile. Hast thou ever heard that friend and foe should abide in one heart? Cast out then the stranger, that the Friend may enter His home.

27

O SON OF DUST!

All that is in heaven and earth I have ordained for thee, except the human heart, which I have made the habitation of My beauty and glory; yet thou didst give My home and dwelling to another than Me; and whenever the manifestation of My holiness sought His own abode, a stranger found He there, and, homeless, hastened unto the sanctuary of the Beloved. Notwithstanding I have concealed thy secret and desire not thy shame.

28

O ESSENCE OF DESIRE!

At many a dawn have I turned from the realms of the Placeless unto thine abode, and found thee on the bed of ease busied with others than Myself. Thereupon, even as the flash of the spirit, I returned to the realms of celestial glory and breathed it not in My retreats above unto the hosts of holiness.

29

O SON OF BOUNTY!

Out of the wastes of nothingness, with the clay of My command, I made thee to appear, and have ordained for thy training every atom in existence and the essence of all created things. Thus, ere thou didst issue from thy mother's womb, I destined for thee two founts of gleaming milk, eyes to watch over thee, and hearts to love thee. Out of My loving-kindness, 'neath the shade of My mercy I nurtured thee, and guarded thee by the essence of My grace and favour. And My purpose in all this was that thou mightest attain My everlasting dominion and become worthy of My invisible bestowals. And yet heedless thou didst remain, and when fully grown, thou didst neglect all My bounties and occupied thyself with thine idle imaginings, in such wise that thou didst become wholly forgetful, and, turning away from the portals of the Friend, didst abide within the courts of My enemy.

30

O BOND SLAVE OF THE WORLD!

Many a dawn hath the breeze of My loving-kindness wafted over thee and found thee upon the bed of heedlessness fast asleep. Bewailing then thy plight it returned whence it came.

31

O SON OF EARTH!

Wouldst thou have Me, seek none other than Me; and wouldst thou gaze upon My beauty, close thine eyes to the world and all that is therein; for My will and the will of another than Me, even as fire and water, cannot dwell together in one heart.

32

O BEFRIENDED STRANGER!

The candle of thine heart is lighted by the hand of My power, quench it not with the contrary winds of self and passion. The healer of all thine ills is remembrance of Me, forget it not. Make My love thy treasure and cherish it even as thy very sight and life.

33

O MY BROTHER!

Hearken to the delightsome words of My honeyed tongue, and quaff the stream of mystic holiness from My sugar-shedding lips. Sow the seeds of My divine wisdom in the pure soil of thy heart, and water them with the water of certitude, that the hyacinths of My knowledge and wisdom may spring up fresh and green in the sacred city of thy heart.

34

O DWELLERS OF MY PARADISE!

With the hands of loving-kindness I have planted in the holy garden of paradise the young tree of your love and friendship, and have watered it with the goodly showers of My tender grace; now that the hour of its fruiting is come, strive that it may be protected, and be not consumed with the flame of desire and passion.

35

O MY FRIENDS!

Quench ye the lamp of error, and kindle within your hearts the everlasting torch of divine guidance. For ere long the assayers of mankind shall, in the holy presence of the Adored, accept naught but purest virtue and deeds of stainless holiness.

36

O SON OF DUST!

The wise are they that speak not unless they obtain a hearing, even as the cup-bearer, who proffereth not his cup till he findeth a seeker, and the lover who crieth not out from the depths of his heart until he gazeth upon the beauty of his beloved. Wherefore sow the seeds of wisdom and knowledge in the pure soil of the heart, and keep them hidden, till the hyacinths of divine wisdom spring from the heart and not from mire and clay.

In the first line of the Tablet it is recorded and written,
and within the sanctuary of the tabernacle of God
is hidden:

37

O MY SERVANT!

Abandon not for that which perisheth an everlasting dominion, and cast not away celestial sovereignty for a worldly desire. This is the river of everlasting life that hath flowed from the well-spring of the pen of the merciful; well is it with them that drink!

38

O SON OF SPIRIT!

Burst thy cage asunder, and even as the phoenix of love soar into the firmament of holiness. Renounce thyself and, filled with the spirit of mercy, abide in the realm of celestial sanctity.

39

O OFFSPRING OF DUST!

Be not content with the ease of a passing day, and deprive not thyself of everlasting rest. Barter not the garden of eternal delight for the dust-heap of a mortal world. Up from thy prison ascend unto the glorious meads above, and from thy mortal cage wing thy flight unto the paradise of the Placeless.

40

O MY SERVANT!

Free thyself from the fetters of this world, and loose thy soul from the prison of self. Seize thy chance, for it will come to thee no more.

41

O SON OF MY HANDMAID!

Didst thou behold immortal sovereignty, thou wouldst strive to pass from this fleeting world. But to conceal the one from thee and to reveal the other is a mystery which none but the pure in heart can comprehend.

42

O MY SERVANT!

Purge thy heart from malice and, innocent of envy,

enter the divine court of holiness.

43

O MY FRIENDS!

Walk ye in the ways of the good pleasure of the

Friend, and know that His pleasure is in the pleasure of His creatures.

That is: no man should enter the house of his friend save at his friend's

pleasure, nor lay hands upon his treasures nor prefer his own will to his

friend's, and in no wise seek an advantage over him. Ponder this,

ye that have insight!

44

O COMPANION OF MY THRONE!

Hear no evil, and see no evil, abase not thyself, neither sigh and weep. Speak no evil, that thou mayest not hear it spoken unto thee, and magnify not the faults of others that thine own faults may not appear great; and wish not the abasement of anyone, that thine own abasement be not exposed. Live then the days of thy life, that are less than a fleeting moment, with thy mind stainless, thy heart unsullied, thy thoughts pure, and thy nature sanctified, so that, free and content, thou mayest put away this mortal frame, and repair unto the mystic paradise and abide in the eternal kingdom for evermore.

45

ALAS! ALAS! O LOVERS OF WORLDLY DESIRE!

Even as the swiftness of lightning ye have passed by the Beloved One, and have set your hearts on satanic fancies. Ye bow the knee before your vain imagining, and call it truth. Ye turn your eyes towards the thorn, and name it a flower. Not a pure breath have ye breathed, nor hath the breeze of detachment been wafted from the meadows of your hearts. Ye have cast to the winds the loving counsels of the Beloved and have effaced them utterly from the tablet of your hearts, and even as the beasts of the field, ye move and have your being within the pastures of desire and passion.

46

O BRETHREN IN THE PATH!

Wherefore have ye neglected the mention of the Loved One, and kept remote from His holy presence? The essence of beauty is within the peerless pavilion, set upon the throne of glory, whilst ye busy yourselves with idle contentions. The sweet savours of holiness are breathing and the breath of bounty is wafted, yet ye are all sorely afflicted and deprived thereof. Alas for you and for them that walk in your ways and follow in your footsteps!

47

O CHILDREN OF DESIRE!

Put away the garment of vainglory, and divest yourselves of the attire of haughtiness.

In the third of the most holy lines writ and recorded
in the Ruby Tablet by the pen of the unseen this
is revealed:

48

O BRETHREN!

Be forbearing one with another and set not your affections on things below. Pride not yourselves in your glory, and be not ashamed of abasement. By My beauty! I have created all things from dust, and to dust will I return them again.

49

O CHILDREN OF DUST!

Tell the rich of the midnight sighing of the poor, lest heedlessness lead them into the path of destruction, and deprive them of the Tree of Wealth. To give and to be generous are attributes of Mine; well is it with him that adorneth himself with My virtues.

50

O QUINTESSENCE OF PASSION!

Put away all covetousness and seek contentment; for the covetous hath ever been deprived, and the contented hath ever been loved and praised.

51

O SON OF MY HANDMAID!

Be not troubled in poverty nor confident in riches, for poverty is followed by riches and riches are followed by poverty. Yet to be poor in all save God is a wondrous gift, belittle not the value thereof, for in the end it will make thee rich in God, and thus thou shalt know the meaning of the utterance, "In truth ye are the poor," and the holy words, "God is the all-possessing," shall even as the true morn break forth gloriously resplendent upon the horizon of the lover's heart, and abide secure on the throne of wealth.

52

O CHILDREN OF NEGLIGENCE AND PASSION!

Ye have suffered My enemy to enter My house and have cast out My friend, for ye have enshrined the love of another than Me in your hearts. Give ear to the sayings of the Friend and turn towards His paradise. Worldly friends, seeking their own good, appear to love one the other, whereas the true Friend hath loved and doth love you for your own sakes; indeed He hath suffered for your guidance countless afflictions. Be not disloyal to such a Friend, nay rather hasten unto Him. Such is the day-star of the word of truth and faithfulness, that hath dawned above the horizon of the pen of the Lord of all names. Open your ears that ye may hearken unto the word of God, the Help in peril, the Self-existent.

53

O YE THAT PRIDE YOURSELVES ON MORTAL RICHES!

Know ye in truth that wealth is a mighty barrier between the seeker and his desire, the lover and his beloved. The rich, but for a few, shall in no wise attain the court of His presence nor enter the city of content and resignation. Well is it then with him, who, being rich, is not hindered by his riches from the eternal kingdom, nor deprived by them of imperishable dominion. By the Most Great Name! The splendour of such a wealthy man shall illuminate the dwellers of heaven even as the sun enlightens the people of the earth!

54

O YE RICH ONES ON EARTH!

The poor in your midst are My trust; guard ye My trust, and be not intent only on your own ease.

55

O SON OF PASSION!

Cleanse thyself from the defilement of riches and in perfect peace advance into the realm of poverty; that from the well-spring of detachment thou mayest quaff the wine of immortal life.

56

O MY SON!

The company of the ungodly increaseth sorrow, whilst fellowship with the righteous cleanseth the rust from off the heart. He that seeketh to commune with God, let him betake himself to the companionship of His loved ones; and he that desireth to hearken unto the word of God, let him give ear to the words of His chosen ones.

57

O SON OF DUST!

Beware! Walk not with the ungodly and seek not fellowship with him, for such companionship turneth the radiance of the heart into infernal fire.

58

O SON OF MY HANDMAID!

Wouldst thou seek the grace of the Holy Spirit, enter into fellowship with the righteous, for he hath drunk the cup of eternal life at the hands of the immortal Cup-bearer and, even as the true morn, doth quicken and illumine the hearts of the dead.

59

O HEEDLESS ONES!

Think not the secrets of hearts are hidden, nay, know ye of a certainty that in clear characters they are engraved and are openly manifest in the holy Presence.

63

O YE PEOPLES OF THE WORLD!

Know, verily, that an unforeseen calamity followeth you, and grievous retribution awaiteth you. Think not that which ye have committed hath been effaced in My sight. By My beauty! All your doings hath My pen graven with open characters upon tablets of chrysolite.

64

O OPPRESSORS ON EARTH!

Withdraw your hands from tyranny, for I have pledged Myself not to forgive any man's injustice. This is My covenant which I have irrevocably decreed in the preserved tablet and sealed it with My seal of glory.

65

O REBELLIOUS ONES!

My forbearance hath emboldened you and My long-suffering hath made you negligent, in such wise that ye have spurred on the fiery charger of passion into perilous ways that lead unto destruction. Have ye thought Me heedless or that I was unaware?

66

O EMIGRANTS!

The tongue I have designed for the mention of Me, defile it not with detraction. If the fire of self overcome you, remember your own faults and not the faults of My creatures, inasmuch as every one of you knoweth his own self better than he knoweth others.

67

O CHILDREN OF FANCY!

Know verily, that while the radiant dawn breaketh above the horizon of eternal holiness, the satanic secrets and deeds done in the gloom of night shall be laid bare and manifest before the peoples of the world.

68

O WEED THAT SPRINGETH OUT OF DUST!

Wherefore have not these soiled hands of thine touched first thine own garment, and why with thine heart defiled with desire and passion dost thou seek to commune with Me and to enter My sacred realm? Far, far are ye from that which ye desire.

69

O CHILDREN OF ADAM!

Holy words and pure and goodly deeds ascend unto the heaven of celestial glory. Strive that your deeds may be cleansed from the dust of self and hypocrisy and find favour at the court of glory; for ere long the assayers of mankind shall, in the holy presence of the Adored One, accept naught but absolute virtue and deeds of stainless purity. This is the day-star of wisdom and of divine mystery that hath shone above the horizon of the divine will. Blessed are they that turn thereunto.

70

O SON OF WORLDLINESS!

Pleasant is the realm of being, wert thou to attain thereto; glorious is the domain of eternity, shouldst thou pass beyond the world of mortality; sweet is the holy ecstacy if thou drinkest of the mystic chalice from the hands of the celestial Youth. Shouldst thou attain this station, thou wouldst be freed from destruction and death, from toil and sin.

71

O MY FRIENDS!

Call ye to mind that covenant ye have entered into with Me upon Mount Paran, situate within the hallowed precincts of Zaman. I have taken to witness the concourse on high and the dwellers in the city of eternity, yet now none do I find faithful unto the covenant. Of a certainty pride and rebellion have effaced it from the hearts, in such wise that no trace thereof remaineth. Yet knowing this, I waited and disclosed it not.

72

O MY SERVANT!

Thou art even as a finely tempered sword concealed in the darkness of its sheath and its value hidden from the artificer's knowledge. Wherefore come forth from the sheath of self and desire that thy worth may be made resplendent and manifest unto all the world.

73

O MY FRIEND!

Thou art the day-star of the heavens of My holiness, let not the defilement of the world eclipse thy splendour. Rend asunder the veil of heedlessness, that from behind the clouds thou mayest emerge resplendent and array all things with the apparel of life.

74

O CHILDREN OF VAINGLORY!

For a fleeting sovereignty ye have abandoned My imperishable dominion, and have adorned yourselves with the gay livery of the world and made of it your boast. By My beauty! All will I gather beneath the one-coloured covering of the dust and efface all these diverse colours save them that choose My own, and that is purging from every colour.

75

O CHILDREN OF NEGLIGENCE!

Set not your affections on mortal sovereignty and rejoice not therein. Ye are even as the unwary bird that with full confidence warbleth upon the bough; till of a sudden the fowler Death throws it upon the dust, and the melody, the form and the colour are gone, leaving not a trace. Wherefore take heed, O bondslaves of desire!

76

O SON OF MY HANDMAID!

Guidance hath ever been given by words, and now it is given by deeds. Every one must show forth deeds that are pure and holy, for words are the property of all alike, whereas such deeds as these belong only to Our loved ones. Strive then with heart and soul to distinguish yourselves by your deeds. In this wise We counsel you in this holy and resplendent tablet.

77

O SON OF JUSTICE!

In the night-season the beauty of the immortal Being hath repaired from the emerald height of fidelity unto the Sadratu'l-Muntahá, and wept with such a weeping that the concourse on high and the dwellers of the realms above wailed at His lamenting. Whereupon there was asked, Why the wailing and weeping? He made reply: As bidden I waited expectant upon the hill of faithfulness, yet inhaled not from them that dwell on earth the fragrance of fidelity. Then summoned to return I beheld, and lo! certain doves of holiness were sore tried within the claws of the dogs of earth. Thereupon the Maid of heaven hastened forth unveiled and resplendent from Her mystic mansion, and asked of their names, and all were told but one. And when urged, the first letter thereof was uttered, whereupon the dwellers of the celestial chambers rushed forth out of their habitation of glory. And whilst the second letter was pronounced they fell down, one and all, upon the dust. At that moment a voice was heard from the inmost shrine: "Thus far and no farther."

Verily We bear witness to that which they have done and now are doing.

78

O SON OF MY HANDMAID!

Quaff from the tongue of the merciful the stream of divine mystery, and behold from the day-spring of divine utterance the unveiled splendour of the day-star of wisdom. Sow the seeds of My divine wisdom in the pure soil of the heart, and water them with the waters of certitude, that the hyacinths of knowledge and wisdom may spring up fresh and green from the holy city of the heart.

79

O SON OF DESIRE!

How long wilt thou soar in the realms of desire? Wings have I bestowed upon thee, that thou mayest fly to the realms of mystic holiness and not the regions of satanic fancy. The comb, too, have I given thee that thou mayest dress My raven locks, and not lacerate My throat.

80

O MY SERVANTS!

Ye are the trees of My garden; ye must give forth goodly and wondrous fruits, that ye yourselves and others may profit therefrom. Thus it is incumbent on every one to engage in crafts and professions, for therein lies the secret of wealth, O men of understanding! For results depend upon means, and the grace of God shall be all-sufficient unto you. Trees that yield no fruit have been and will ever be for the fire.

81

O MY SERVANT!

The basest of men are they that yield no fruit on earth. Such men are verily counted as among the dead, nay better are the dead in the sight of God than those idle and worthless souls.

82

O MY SERVANT!

The best of men are they that earn a livelihood by their calling and spend upon themselves and upon their kindred for the love of God, the Lord of all worlds.

The mystic and wondrous Bride, hidden ere this beneath the veiling of utterance, hath now, by the grace of God and His divine favour, been made manifest even as the resplendent light shed by the beauty of the Beloved. I bear witness, O friends! that the favour is complete, the argument fulfilled, the proof manifest and the evidence established. Let it now be seen what your endeavours in the path of detachment will reveal. In this wise hath the divine favour been fully vouchsafed unto you and unto them that are in heaven and on earth. All praise to God, the Lord of all Worlds.